Kenzi Does It All

Written by

Barbara Alleyne

Kenzi Does It All

iUniverse books may be ordered through booksellers or by contacting:

iUniverse
1663 Liberty Drive
Bloomington, IN 47403
www.iuniverse.com
844-349-9409

Because of the dynamic nature of the Internet, any web addresses or links contained in this book may have changed since publication and may no longer be valid. The views expressed in this work are solely those of the author and do not necessarily reflect the views of the publisher, and the publisher hereby disclaims any responsibility for them.

Any people depicted in stock imagery provided by Getty Images are models, and such images are being used for illustrative purposes only.
Certain stock imagery © Getty Images.

ISBN: 978-1-6632-6226-4 (sc)
978-1-6632-6304-9 (hc)
978-1-6632-6227-1 (e)

Library of Congress Control Number: 2024908059

Print information available on the last page.

iUniverse rev. date: 05/14/2024

Introduction

Come meet the amazingly talented Kenzi G
A star in the making ever since she was three
She likes to do chores way too big for her
So, her parents call her their little helper.

At the age of five she became a girl scout
She participates in all activities done by her troop
Whether its hiking, archery or just taking a swim
Kenzi's aim is to always perform to win.

Several certificates displayed on her bedroom wall
Show each time she was on her school's honor roll
She plays basketball with an aggressive throw
Representing her team as an outstanding pro.

So, come along and follow the story
Of the amazingly talented Kenzi G

Parkway Gardens is buzzing with activity as today marks the beginning of a new school year. It's also the day when the amazingly talented Kenzi G will embark on her journey into first grade.

A school bus stops at the corner where Kenzi and other children are waiting to be taken to school.

Kenzi beams with excitement, thrilled that she will be entering first grade, and looking forward to making new friends.

Everyone is silent as the bus monitor shows them how to securely fasten their seatbelts for the fifteen-minute ride to the school.

5

Kenzi is confident that she will do well in first grade, just as she did while in summer camp, when she quickly learned and mastered the breaststroke and butterfly maneuvers.

As the bus rolls into the schoolyard, silence prevails. Everyone disembarks and quietly awaits further instructions from the bus monitor.

Soon a teacher's aide comes to the bus to greet them.

9

Kenzi is excited to meet her teacher and looks forward to quickly learning all the assignments she will get in class.

11

She is also eager to meet her classmates.

One day, during the first semester, a girl scout recruiter came to the school to recruit young girls for the girl scout program.

Kenzi quickly raised her hand and bravely expressed her desire to become a girl scout.

She was overjoyed when her mom agreed to let her join the Girl Scout program. Subsequently, she was officially registered. Now she would get to participate in all the girl scout activities.

Kenzi relishes every outing she embarks on with her Girl Scout troop. Through these adventures, she has acquired many outdoor skills, honed during memorable camping experiences with her fellow scouts.

17

18

In addition to her academic accomplishments, she has been honored with a Learner Profile Caring award. This recognition is reserved for students who are caring, show empathy, compassion, and respect, demonstrating a steadfast commitment to service and a genuine desire to make a positive impact in the lives of others.

Kenzi's academic achievements in school seem endless. She's been on the honor roll every semester since first grade and she has received numerous awards for her outstanding performances.

Kenzi's commitment to every activity she participates in, her willingness and exceptional ability to help others have earned her praise from both her teachers and peers.

Her eagerness to reach out and help with many tasks knows no bounds.

As a nature lover, Kenzi enjoys all outdoor activities. If you ever pass by her home during the summer months, you might catch a glimpse of Kenzi and her mom tending to the beautiful tulips in their garden.

She says that tulips make her feel happy.

The suburban town where Kenzi and her family live boasts gently sloping hills that dot the landscape sporadically.

Snow falls there quite often during the winter.

One day there was a big snowfall. Snow had fallen since early morning, transforming the surrounding trees into a winter wonderland.

Kenzi's dad had to shovel the snow from the family's driveway to make a path. Kenzi asked him to let her help shovel the snow.

Even though it would have been a big task for her, he let her help a little bit, using her toy shovel. Subsequently, she had fun in the snow. She even made a little snowman ⛄.

Kenzi is involved in several sporting activities such as swimming, playing softball and basketball. Her favorite sport is basketball.

Her dad registered her in a basketball team for young girls.

One day while observing the way she plays basketball, he remarked that she can throw a mean dunk. He also predicted that she will soon master the sport.

Considering all the activities she has been involved in and the skills she has mastered, Kenzi has demonstrated that she will undoubtedly become an outstanding leader in her chosen profession.

This book honors my niece whose talents and exceptional abilities is a shining example of caring and sharing.

Printed in the United States
by Baker & Taylor Publisher Services